To the Hubbard Family
Dr. Naeim Weygant

D0991760

# IT'S SUMMER!

# IT'S SUMMER!

Text
and
Photographs
by
SISTER NOEMI WEYGANT, O.S.B.

THE WESTMINSTER PRESS
Philadelphia

ISBN 0-664-32471-1

LIBRARY OF CONGRESS CATALOG CARD No. 77-104078

BOOK DESIGN BY
DOROTHY ALDEN SMITH

Published by The Westminster Press ®
Philadelphia, Pennsylvania

PRINTED IN THE UNITED STATES OF AMERICA

# CONTENTS

# A TIME FOR PICTURES

SUMMER is a time to be happy and dreamy, a time for quiet idleness and peace. Summer is blue, rose-gold, with cool wind and warm sunlight. Summer is a time for pictures.

The convent where I live was once called "The Daisy Farm," and every summer this persistent, favorite wild flower shows up for me to photograph. Some years the sunflower flourishes too. Other years it has no pictorial value or personality. One year we had a unique red sunflower.

No flower compares to the bleeding heart in beauty or humor. While I have more than once arranged a bouquet for a Feast of the Sacred Heart, this time I had a little fun with it. The buttercup bewitches me, and I have photographed dozens, alone or in clusters, in meadows, along woodlands, or beside streams.

Many photographers stay out of the woods right after a rain because the scene is wet and dull, but at such moments I have found many pictures otherwise lost: a jeweled tongue, a pink blossom upside down on a green rock, a row of diamonds on a bending blade of grass!

Slime molds create beautiful colors, but you must get their pictures quickly, for soon their loveliness goes and they are left brown, drying. Although I can hardly name one fungus there are so many varieties, their color and their imagery are a constant endearing surprise. "Humbug" was really a fungus that exploded one cold night. In black and white his picture won a National Award.

Whenever I pursue a butterfly with the camera, I know how slight is my chance of success, but the chase is a delight. To get a picture of a dragonfly I must stand alone, motionless, in an area where they are landing and taking off in numbers, always ready to snap a picture. They are so swift and graceful—except the guy on page 36! Spider webs are witchy to take, but a triumph to capture.

I could scarcely believe the Sister who told me there was

a weed down by the creek I had not photographed. I have haunted our woodlands so avidly year after year with the camera. But she was right. I came home with a picture of a variety of horsetail never found there before or since. We have not many nut trees in our part of Minnesota, but the hazel is common on our convent grounds, and fun to photograph. The picture of the wasp nest I took with the first telephoto lense I ever owned, not a very powerful one, so I felt terribly brave and immensely excited.

Experience has taught me that the trick is not what camera to use, but the use to which you put the camera you have. You must stay within its limitations, at the same time making it work to its full potential. This you discover by using it. I always encourage a student never to give up one camera for another until he is boss of the camera he has.

The Kalimar six/sixty became my favorite, not because it is the best camera available, but because it offers a good-sized negative to work with and, at very low cost, three extension rings for extreme closeup work. Yet at times the Kalimar is too big, too clumsy, too slow. So I always take a 35mm. camera too out in the field—either the Contaflex with a set of closeup lenses or a Leicaflex. I have a Beseler enlarger in the darkroom, and for copy work in the studio I use an old faithful 4 x 5 Speed Graphic.

I never hold a camera, old or new, without cherishing it, without excitement, because I am so indebted to photography for enriching my life, for keeping it adventurous and beautiful and meaningful. So, too, the smell of the acid fixer in the darkroom remains sweet to me, for it is there in the dark that the pictures I have taken in light come to life, and the wonder of it all never ceases.

*Sister Noemi Weygant*

# SUMMER IS HAPPY, DREAMY, BUSY

Come, children,
    off we go
        to the woodlands and meadows
    with a lunch pack,
        and no rush
        about getting back.

Summer is a chance
    to find out more
        about the world you live in—
And how good
    is living!

# DAISY TIME

In the meadow
  the daisies,
    high, low,
    in bright,
    in shadow,
  are having
    a party.

Their short dresses
  are made of petals
  satin white,
    and fitted tight
    about the waist.
Each fold
  is sprinkled
  with gold.

Run, run
  into the daisies.
For the summer day,
  honey tasting,
  calls out to you
  to roll down a hill
    in grasses that tickle,
  to take off your shoes
    and let your toes wiggle . . .

Then, lying flat on your back,
  watch the white clouds waltzing,
  for on you, and everything,
    a blue sky is smiling.

# TO HEAR HIS HEARTBEAT

Oh,
how often
I have tried
to catch
a butterfly.

Many times,
chasing him,
I have begged him—
please—
to let me
hold him
in my open hand,
so that I
might feel him,
velvety,
walking over it,
and find joy
in his beauty.

While holding him,
I would also like,
because he is
so swift
in flight,
to listen
to his heartbeat.

I would never
hurt him,
but he will never
trust me.

# AWAITING THE COUNTDOWN

A pine tree
   is nearly ready
      to send up
      another missile.

The missile's
   gold tip
      is headed
      for the blue.
And the needles
   of the pine
      serve as
      a  launching  crew.

# SHARE A WILD ROSE

Summer is never
  quite here
  until the wild rose
    appears.
As I put
  my face into it,
    tears come to my eyes.
I wonder why?

The wild rose doesn't
  smell nearly
  as pretty
    as the tame rose.

And though tame roses
  last for days
    in water,
  the petals
  of the wild rose
    are falling
    onto the dinner table
  even before father
  has come home
  to see what
  I picked for him
    as a surprise.

# WHAT IN THE WORLD?

Are these clay pipes
   for men to smoke
      around a conference table?

Or are they the spears
   of African natives?

Have they been painted
   by an artist,
   or are these the colors
      God gave them?

Are they hollow inside,
   so that little boys,
     taking off their heads,
   can use them
     for pebble shooters:
   or little girls
     can drop threads
     through the tubes
   and wear them
     for necklaces?

# FLOWER OR BIRD?

Is this a flower?
No, obviously,
   it's a bird
    that has been feathered
     and awaits the broiler.

As for its name—
   all naked,
   beheaded birds
    look the same!

# BUTTERCUP FIRE

Here's a golden goblet
   for holding wine,
     a little saucer
     for catching rain,
   a sundial
   for telling time.

Often,
   near a dark forest,
   it burns
     with a yellow,
     waxy flame,
   though it has never set
   a woods on fire.

So dainty
   on a long stem,
     it sways brightly
   in a wind
     for hours and hours,
     and never tires.

This favorite flower
   waits to tell
     whether
   you like butter.

# HAZEL

Her name is Hazel,
   and when she looks
   into the mirror
   of the sky
      with her twinkle eyes—
   she thinks she's beautiful.

Insects use her nose
   for a slide.
Then after—
   they complain
   she's bristly
   and positively dangerous
      when she sneezes.
But she doesn't mind
   their ingratitude.

What really upsets her
   is when people,
   passing by,
      call her a nut,
   for she knows
      that's no compliment.

So, laying her head
   on her green-gold pillow,
   she cries until her nose
      gets red and blurry.

# JEWELED TONGUE

One leaf,
    wet with rain,
       becomes
    a jeweled tongue,
    and captures
    a blossom
       upon which to dine.

But if the leaf
    wants to finish its treat,
       it must hurry.

The sun is about to
    lick up
       the rain,
    and the flower
       will fall away
       into cool shade.

# IS THIS A FIRE?

Is this a pond lily
   blowing bubbles?
     Or a crater
     erupting?

Most certainly,
   there is fire
   inside that cavity.
Why doesn't the water
   on which the crater floats,
     put out
     the fire?

# WHOOPEE!

Want a horseback ride?
Fine!
Won't cost you a dime.

Jump
   into the saddle
      made of fungus-hide
   and go galloping
      round the stump.
Every knot
   gives you
   a jolly good bump.

Whoopee!

# WHAT KIND OF LIZARD?

What kind of lizard
    did the rain
    drop down upon
    this leaf?

Will he return
    to the sky,
    or fall beneath,
    with a silver quiver?

# BEWARE

This nest hangs
   like a lovely
   paper basket
   among the green leaves
   of a young tree.
Beware!
Its beauty deceives.

A wasp queen
   and her colony
   live there,
     and never,
     to anyone,
     or to anything,
   have they ever
   offered hospitality.

# DISGRACEFUL

Such a landing!
Shame!
Are you not aware
 that you have a name
 to live up to?

The dragonfly
 is thought to be
 one of the
 most graceful
 insects in flight.
And here you are,
 a disgraceful sight!

# SLINGSHOT

Here's a slingshot
   made from weed.

The band
   that spans
   the fork
     was spun by a spider.

For shooting,
   use old berries.

Maybe it won't
   last long
   in a little boy's hands,
     but you can
     find out . . .

## LADY CLOVER

Here's a silken
　　lady clover, pursued
　　by many an insect rover.

She glistens
　　in the sun,
　　　lacy,
　　　slim.
She wears a
　　purple wig,
　　and dances
　　an Irish jig
　　　with the wind.

# SHE WALKS RED FIRE

She comes from
   a gold moon,
      and walks red fire.

She drinks sweet nectar
   from a burning flower.

She helps
   make royal jelly
      for the queen.

And sings in the sun,
   hummmmmmmm . . .

# THREE CANDLES

When, going
    through a forest,
    you find
    three slender candles
        that appear
        to have been
        blown out
        by a wind . . .

Then you know
    you are treading
    the tracks
        of a deer.

He walked by
    not long ago
        and dined on tender greens.

Where is he?

Listen!

All you hear
    is silence.

All you see
    is sunlight passing
    through the leaves.

# JEWELS IN THE VELVET GRASS

The rarest necklaces
   in the world
   are made by rain,
      stringing beads
      upon the threads
   of spider webs.

After a shower
   they adorn
      each field flower.

Oh,
   how we wish
      to wear them!

# HUMBUG

He walks down
  a blue log
    with sticky paws.

He has a broad tail,
  a little snout,
    and the markings
    of a wild animal.

Do you know what plant,
  bird,
  or wild creature
    he pretends to be?

# WHAT STRANGE BIRD?

These surely must be
    the eggs
        of a wild bird!

But so many!

And
    the shell
        is so sandpapery!

The eggs
    vary so
        in size,
    and push
    each other
        into such odd shapes.

When you
    squeeze one,
        does its shell break?
Or does it go your way
    like rubber,
    or clay?

# CAN YOU TELL ME?

Why should a sunflower
  ever appear
  to be a
  squeeze-open,
    quick-change purse?

The sunflower
  will never need
  a token
    for a ride.

Even though
  it gazes daily
  into the sky,
  it will never
  go anywhere,
    except as the wind
    blows it
    to the right,
    to the left.

And surely
  it would never
  wish to buy
  a candy bar,
    for already it's so sweet
    the bees are ever
    after its honey.

So, can you tell me
  why a sunflower
    would ever need
    a nickel or a dime?

# FOUR AND TWENTY

Four and twenty blackbirds
baked in a pie. . . .
Blueberries, too, are birdy,
and baked in a pie.

# BREAKFAST

This must be
  a place to eat.
Three pancakes
  already await
    the next customer.

The cook, however,
  must not be good,
  for don't the cakes
  look more thick
  and heavy
    than they should?

And where
  is the syrup?

# RESOURCEFUL

At night
   he works
   to weave
   a strong web
   in which to bag
   a grasshopper
      with his own brand
      of cellophane.

Then,
   he roasts it
   in the sun
   for dinner dining,
      while he catches up
      on his sleep.

The mattress,
   of his own designing,
   is soft and white
   as foam,
      with a little ladder
      running down
      toward the ground.

# LAST SUMMER

Last summer
   a little girl and boy
   came to the lake
     and found a dish to hold
     pretty pebbles.

One day
   the little girl said,
   "Let us play house,
   and I'll make you
   a dinner."
     So the dish became a platter.

Upon the shell
   the little girl
   put a snail,
   a hot dog,
   and other sticks
   of meat
     and laid them
     in the sun
     to cook.

Then the children
   were called
   to their cabin
     and they never
     came back to eat.

# SUMMER IS DREAM TIME

A white bowl,
  golden fire inside,
  is floating
  in the reflection
  of the sky
    with a satin leaf
    folded beneath.

Jump out of your boat.
Like a frog leap
  from one big leaf
    to another.

Suddenly,
  breathless,
  drop onto a pad—
    leathery, cool.
Curl up and nap.

When you awaken,
  look about—
  surprised.
Yawn, stretch,
  and jump again
  into the boat
  that has been waiting
  for your dream,
    for all summer dreams,
    to end.

Very soon now, fall begins,
  and school.